1E

Would be lovely to meet you in person again.

The Last Almanac

Best Wishes

Bob Beagrie

Bob

© Copyright Bob Beagrie, 2023
Published by Yaffle Press, 2023

https://www.yafflepress.co.uk/

All rights reserved. No part of this book may be copied, reproduced, stored in a retrieval system or transmitted, in any form or by any electronic or mechanical means without the prior permission of the copyright holder.

ISBN:	978-1-913122-34-8
Cover image:	Bob Beagrie
Author photograph:	Courtesy of Kev Howard
Cover design:	Mike Farren
Editing:	Mike Farren
Typesetting:	Mike Farren

Acknowledgements

Thanks go to the editors of the following magazines, journals, anthologies and chapbooks in which some of these poems and earlier versions of them have previously been published: *Nobody* (Hunting Raven Press), *Co-Incidental 03* (The Black Light Engine Room), *Light* (The Black Light Engine Room), *Double Bill: Poems Inspired by Popular Culture* (Red Squirrel Press), *Solstice Shorts* (Arachne Press), *Building Bridges Anthology* (Ek Zuban), *Up the Duff* (Beautiful Dragons), *Interpreter's House, Envoi, Bare Fiction, Raum, Obsessed With Pipework, Sarasvati, Wilderness House Literary Review, New Reader Magazine, Earth Shadow Poetry, Honest Ulsterman, The Linnet's Wings, Dreamcatcher, The Lake Poetry Webzine, Lothlorien Poetry Journal, The Blue Nib, One Hand Clapping, The Pangolin Review, Stepaway,*

Poetry Scotland, Spelt, Dodging the Rain, Southlight, 14 Magazine, Fragmented Voices, The Flying Dodo and *Dodging the Rain.*

'To Charm a River' was commissioned by River Tees Rediscovered. 'Dog-Day' was placed third in the Dear Politicians Ecopoetry Competition. Some of the poems in this collection have been recorded with accompanying music as part of Project Lono,

https://soundcloud.com/projectlono-1

https://projectlono.bandcamp.com/

Thanks also go to Stewart Forth for our long friendship and creative collaborations.

Contents:

First Quarter

Seeding the Solstice	3
Fairy Lore from Middridge	4
Snow Song	5
Something Like but Not Quite Purpose	6
Spirits	7
The Red String	8
It's like...	9
The Glow	10
Mem-U Zin	11
The Dark Mile	12
Evensong	14
Imbolc	15
The Backend of Winter	16
North Gare	17
The Weatherers	18
House-bound	19
Persephone	20
Quiet in the House	22
Tees Song	23
Not Only This	24
Sympathy for the Night	25
The Details Burn	26
Ei Mitään	27
To Charm a River	28
Watching the Witch	30
The Handfasting	31

Second Quarter

Spell	33
Life Lessons	34
Message	35
Shade	36
Triskelion	38
Today's Threads	39
Good Friday	40
The Trail Back	41
Big Sea	42
Rose Tinted Rhapsody	44
Sunshine After the Shower	45
A Tub of Nostalgia	46
Tai Qi Among the Crows	48
Caught in the DC Multiverse	49
Film	50
Hand and Arm	51
Curved Form (Delphi)	53
Kirkcarrion	54
Beyond the Flesh	56
The Jig of Life	57
Those Tubes that Carry Messages	58
Tincture	59
Witchtide	61

Third Quarter

Beltane	63
Chaffinch Among the Daffodils	65
Abracadabra	66
The old cow shed	67
Sheepwash	68
The Nine Sisters	69
Everything Under the Sun	70
Splendere	72
The Birthing	73
Creation Myth	74
Noctilucent Clouds	75
Tat Tvam Asi	76
Watching Swallows at Ludworth Tower	77
Misprediction	80
Hide and Seek	81
Horseshoe Bend, Thornaby	82
Border Blessing	84
Dunbar Dream-Song	85
Old Uncle Tay	87
Measurements	88
Water Feature Beside the Bottle of Notes	89
Dog-Day	90
Rift Woods	92
Re-Wilding	93
Holding Liquid	95
Gorge Tide	96
At Odds	97
The Man in The Moon	98
Kite Over Morton Castle	100
Pareidolia	101
Anti-climax	103

Fourth Quarter

Lammas Rain	105
Vanishing Point	106
Love Me Tender	107
The Jackpot	109
Film Poem	110
Premonition	112
The Hand of Glory	114
Mabon	116
Triangulation	117
Local Legend	118
Groundlings	119
Walking the Dog	121
Hardraw	122
Samhain	124
Burning the Bones	125
Wild Route	126
Headland	128
Head of the Heathen	130
Christ on a Stick	132
Pheasants in Porvoo Snow	134
Brief Visitor	135
Unrealing Ontology, 2016	136
Driftwood	137
The Reunion	138
Meeting the *Cailleach*	140
Herd	141
Dunking for a New Sun	142

For Levi

"The almanac of time, hangs in the brain;
The seasons numbered, by the inward sun,"

DYLAN THOMAS

"Call the world if you Please, 'the vale of Soul-making'."

JOHN KEATS

First Quarter

"In the bleak midwinter, frosty wind made moan,
Earth stood hard as iron, water like a stone;"

CHRISTINA ROSSETTI

Seeding the Solstice

Here, once, there was a storytelling throne
but now the way over the bridge is barred
by ranks of tall, tufted grasses, ash and beech
have retreated behind a thumb-smudged sky.
This wee glen clings fast to their tap roots,
it's warm in these woods for this time of year,
no snow, nor hoar-laced twigs, not one puddle
wearing a plate of ice, but so spaciously still
between the damp trunks, each gap a stage
in waiting, at the heart of the dell is a pond
that floats the low sun's sinking face within
a frame of moss, fallen leaves, snail shells,
moorhen feather, around which we've come
to scatter our swollen parts like the decaying
galaxies of crab apples to let both sourness
and sweetness season the soil from which
we hope to grow with each lengthening day.

Fairy Lore from Middridge

At the post-Christmas party, the old drunk told me,
*You know, it's never safe to see yourself reflected
in the slit pupils of fairies, nor to hear your voice
through their tapered ears, muted by pulse drums
in dark canals, it's unwise to dance their dances
to their bells, flutes, pipes in their soft pixie shoes,
or even barefoot on the grass, and to ring-a-roses
widdershins around a ring of toadstools could see
you sealed inside it, almost invisible but for a sperm
stain in moonlight, and do not admit you do not
believe in the Faie even as you wrench at Oberon's
lance that has pierced your door, for deep down
you know, right now, they're standing behind us,
unperceivable in mirrors like your own mind's eye.*

Snow Song

These snowflakes have come so far and long
to drift, quivering, as thumbnail galaxies
out from the downy sky to kiss your cheeks,
make you blink with each delicate drumbeat
and dissolve to nothing upon your tongue
as you stand still, listening to its swaddling –
that quiet melody that pulls perspectives
apart, demands we all take things slower,
consider our habits, step with extra care,
its tempo teaches how to walk with ghosts.

Something Like but Not Quite Purpose

The early evening darkness makes the compressed
voices of the rattlers at the alley gate reverberate
down the street as they wait for the dealer to appear
from behind the steel bins with a pocketful of brief
forgetfulness, and while I wait for you to get home
from the job that's coming to an end as you know it,
up on Eston Hills kids are lighting fires like beacons
to warn of the Spanish Armada, and the last blast
furnace at Teesmouth is being demolished, mam's
skinny feet are throbbing with arthritis – she learned
to swim among slag heaps near the Gare but hates
the creeping signs of old age and Dad's increasing
deafness is one of his secret comforts; everyone is
getting back into the grind, going dry, hitting their
own treadmill, looking forward, glancing back,
the solid spaces around each of us have been painted
by Vermeer, the wind is keening its bitter woes
in the chimney and while looking for the wet wipes
under the sofa I have found a new word but have no
idea what it means, soft and fresh as a snowbell,
fragile as a newly hatched chick, potent as an ink cap
shroom, it's been growing there, I think, since New
Year's Day and it stains my cupped hand like a freshly
plucked heart as I hold it up to the lamplight, leaking
a drop of sticky sap with each shored instinctual beat.

Spirits

Up on the bank
hardly discernible
among the tree trunks
and gathering gloom
two deer stand
watching as we pass
following the path
back to our parked car,
still as boulders
but I sense the quick-
fire-flicker of flight
in their stance, should
we move toward them,
ready to bolt and vanish
like two dark flames
into nowhere,
but we just stand,
breathing, held
within their gaze
their hearing, their noses
twitching, they are
taking us in, forming
us in their sleek skulls,
weighing us in the warm
chambers of their animal
hearts, as we do
with them, and I measure
them almost lighter
than this dank wood-
land air, as weightless
as moonlight and shade
but solid enough to carry
behind my eyes
all the way back
to our hearth.

The Red String

Frost on the rooftiles;
the low afternoon
tongues the grooves.
Pleasure, tell me again,
twice over, so it will go in
this time, the legend
of the string of fate
in which our bodies
grow as transparent
as whispers, except
for the forest of veins
reaching beyond
what we think of as skin.
I make a pinky truce
with the fading light:
to wait for its return.
It tries to hang around
a few moments longer
but it slips on thin ice
off the sugar-coated roof.

It's like…

I'm dying of hypothermia,
she says, in a Gateshead filling station,
where the heater's packed in
even though it's just been fixed,
though she's loving the fact
that she can smell again
after two long weeks of bunged-up flu
especially as that fit workman
in oil-stained orange overalls
smells so sweetly of peaches.

The Glow

With our new school waiting on the far side
of the playing field, pillowed by freezing fog,
we sat on the rug by her feet, following the ride
of Mam's words from the dog-eared paperback
perched in her hand as we spooned dollops
of Ready Brek into our mouths, staring
at the band of glowing red spiralling
along the single bar behind the grill,
while she read out the next chapter all about
some character overcoming adversity, the warmth
in her voice melting frost's morning scriptures
on the pane, the sky behind Jack's foliage,
I think it was pink, as her voice led us
through the trials of this tale, licked fingers
turning corners of pages to the next
impending cliff hanger where she'd stop,
*That's all for now. No ifs, no buts, it's time
you two get into your coats, hats and gloves.*
High time we got out from under her feet,
to head off, leaving twin trails of footprints
across the iced-brittle grass of the pitches.

*Mem U Zin**

The mountain crags of Kurdistan
loom over Parliament Road today
as shawarma rotate on fixed orbits
beneath the flat we used to rent
and Mem and Zin re-choreograph
a tragic epic of eternal separation,
between flurries the nether sun
graffities its tag on topped-up snow,
and ice shards in the fish monger's
window, spilling over red snappers,
bass, crevettes, our breaths become
flags, heraldic emblems: doves,
dragons, skull and crossbones,
and the mirage crags of Kurdistan
cast Newport Bridge in shadow –
both being mere icons of home,
as we bang bumpers, slip and slide
on the beast's shaken off scales,
its horns, buried in each of us,
are what's keeping us all apart.

*Mem and Zin is a Kurdish classic love story written down 1692 and is considered to be the *épopée* of Kurdish literature. It is the most important work of Kurdish writer and poet Ahmad Khani. The content is similar to a Romeo and Juliet story.

The Dark Mile
(for Luke Harding)

At this time of year if you stop,
you'll stiffen up,

the sweat of your labours
will soon chill,

night winds will steal your breath,
whatever the reason

you're on this path in the first place
will freeze

along with the cogs of your resolve,
you'll shiver,

for a while at least, the rocky ground
will appear feather-soft,

the moors, flickering in a wolf moon
and scudding cloud

will wax a memory of a black
and white film,

a Sunday matinee from the age
of analogue

half-watched from the sofa
after dinner,

the desolate track cutting across
the stone- and bone-

strewn fell is full of spectres:
grisly farm hands,

lost legionnaires, vagrants, witches,
chieftains shambling

from round barrows, walking morts,
they haul constellations

of entropy like bluestones
on wooden runners,

bickering in croaks about what's best,
whether you should

stay and rest or unearth the reserves
to get off your arse

and force your bruised soles on
to pound the gravel

for another mile, one more mile,
just another dark mile.

Evensong

Gibbous moon latched by a dream catcher
crooning the blues over snow-swaddled hills
where towns and villages break like waves
in the curtain twitch of isolating suburbs;
the holy watchfulness of the little egret
perched upon a bare branch over the gill
with the patience of basking ivy leaves,
its own pale smudge snagged amid debris
going nowhere fast in the cold lunar flood
the yearly catastrophes of freeze and melt
clogged drains gargling fresh darknesses,
the waters glow with living room lamps;
she sails twilight in her threadbare shawl
the ancient parade of the not-yet-born
between day's demise and hatchling night
the sky is like the wide-open sea, gone quiet
lulled at last from turbulence, laid out
across thickening mirk, a dropping away,
as she dips her slippered feet into skull cups
of sleep, skips over white moors to Swainby.

Imbolc

I'm struggling to remember
the warm face of the sun,
but it's there somewhere
in the bottom drawer of my brain
like a stroke of the most familiar
hand when I woke from rotten,
shuddering fever dreams
and a voice known from before
sense memory formed, in that time
before our counted time began,
but in this beautiful, bleak world
of bare bark, twig fingers, mud,
low freezing mists, slow
occurrences are occurring
in their own good time, so many
ordinary miracles unfolding
beneath the surface of this dumb,
anesthetized crust, underneath
the numb throbbing, the cracking
of stiffened water, those pangs
for sameness, is that hoary
soreness for what we will inevitably
become, whatever it is we
happen to carry, shed, pass on.

The Backend of Winter

Slumber-starved darkness
spilling down the hillside,
pinprick glares on the watch
for lone walkers, through
insomnia-scaffolded lids –

(did we misplace the dreaming elsewhere)

A girl in an institutional
corridor casts a silhouetted
S.O.S through ever-receding
windows, floating within
an air-conditioned bubble –

(so we displace the dreaming elsewise)

The aftertaste of sunshine
on stubborn patches of snow
cradled in the cup of my tongue
burns off on the tip of a flare-
stack, runs off into the river –

(dreaming the streams of elsewhence)

North Gare

Cormorants at the mouth
dive in little arcs and vanish,
cat paws dapple the billows,
layers of crumbling concrete
poured upon Cnut's crumbling
concrete, jagged teeth, metal
fillings, bits of broken boats,
crab-pots, obsolete machinery;
everyone ignores
the 'NO PUBLIC ACCESS' sign,
the 'DANGER – UNSAFE STRUCTURE' sign
and slips around the fence like us
black cormorants swimming
in my mouth testing the depths
churning the swell and hunting
for what it's still possible to say;
where will they resurface?
Waiting, it comes on suddenly
this feathery feeling as tankers
sail into my eyes, I'm sure
if I close them tight, they'll never
reach the open sea so we might
shore them up, lulled by the slap
and shush of the river's pulse,
sunshine on my face rosy
through closed lids, salt
breeze uncommonly warm
carries us over the curvature.

The Weatherers

We could talk about the first flush of blossom
spotting the dark-stripped twigs like cool sparks
or a far star cluster inching closer by the day,
we could mention the flutter of hope they bring
the imperceptible melting but Winter has made
us stoic and silent as lichen. We have languished,
after all, in the House of Patience, know its gradients,
the uneven laminate, mould growth beneath
the damp course, having hunkered down between
the grains in a bristle of living too slow to note,
frictioned between eras and empires. We
could share our thoughts but our lips are sewn
too tight for those kinds of words, they clog
our throats like fur balls – we can eat and drink
(we are ingenious) and there are things inside
or beneath us that know how to survive
if we dare to listen, at times when there's no one
else to listen to but everyone is blabbering
with so much to say, a wind-song spillage
that evaporates, for our lips are sewn up too tight
for the deep words, the slow words of nourishment,
that creep across bare stone in camouflaged frills,
peeling flakes, so it'll take more than a faint
tinge of pink, clusters of snowdrops on verges
for us to shed any of our layers, to soften
the stance we've learned, through endurance,
to hold by embracing the cold and the trembling.

House-bound

Daylight exhaling from out of the room,
shadow pools spread from the far corners
outside, beyond nets that catch nothing,
this end of the street is gathering dusk,
a lad cycles by, no hands, lights switch on
and curtains are drawn in all the homes
opposite, bubbles of a rising argument
in a language of springs and wells, her voice
shrill as a lifeboat siren, the streetlights
blink on in synchronicity, from up on high
the new Street-Cam makes its observations
not noticing the sky holding on to blue,
sitting, like a cat, watching at the window
I listen for the familiar sound of your car.

Persephone

As yet, no sign of her though the days
are getting noticeably longer, the nights
we carry, especially those inside us,
seem denser with the sedimentary
darkness of accumulated Winter

like compacted snow

ice-bonded to a solidity too hard
to make angel impressions with your own

prostrated body, and I realise
I have it all wrong, like most things,
that these sooty nights are also
hers, as well as each of ours,

Nights of the Dead seeping in
from our Underworlds,

where she sits in the throne room
with its eternal fleshless nocturnes,
itching to put on a different mask,
slip out and follow worm tunnels
into rabbit burrows and crawl out
into sun-warmed, wind-sung air.

Just look at her, her eyes are hollow,
poor love, and judging by the scabs
on her arms she's self-harming again

(who can blame her?)

does she even remember the body-
heat of another's skin against hers?

There are a few pink pomegranate
seeds still to digest before
she can re-cross the Black River
and steer us all back to the flame
that smoulders on within the egg.

In the meantime, hear her crisp wail,
*Patience my children, you must first
learn to love and hold this bleakness,
find peace in the keenness of my rage.*

Quiet in the House

Sunlight sings basso profundo
to the soubrette of shadow,
at the loose end of a morning
when it's hard to settle upon
any one thing because
all objects are in transition,
calling *hello, goodbye*;

> leather sofa to mantle
> cabinet to bookshelf

as I drift between coffee
and cigarettes, from one
book to the next to the hairy
hum of a lazy bluebottle's
reconnaissance roaming;

> window to stairwell
> kitchen to curtain

charting the swell of matter,
droning *how do, farewell*
flashing green, electric blue,
waves of water, sound, wind;
while waiting for nothing-
letting go of the longing
to keep you fixed and close
when you are all but flown.

Tees Song

Who's to think they could own a river?
Bound by snow drifts and plates of ice –
a surname fixed by dried ink on paper
while its waters run in restlessness.

They cannot spot us as we trudge,
crunching twin trails of footprints
between tall, slender, golden reeds'
tufted heads that quake and quiver.

As the Baltic wind begins to holler,
flings a white gull against its flight
and brings a swirl of dancing flakes
to brush our lashes, tap our cheeks.

As the river hoards pilfered colours
it slithers on toward another sunset
and we, who've trod enough today,
turn back to wander into twilight.

Not Only This

Having stalked the budding, water-gouged crease,
single file, between municipal golf course
and school grounds, still possible to imagine –
as long as you keep your scope myopic,
as forest-wide, the original unhemmed
sprawl of unchartered thought –
where we were startled by the warning clap
of a wood pigeon's wings sharp as a shot
from an air rifle as it rode the draught
over the branch-clogged beck,
where we submitted to the examination
of a lone bee's inquisition,
wishing it well with a nonchalance
bordering on unmentionable hope,
and having paused to ponder
the blackened patches of fire stains,
the tree shrine to a suspected suicide
with its deflated balloons, love hearts,
drying flowers, poems and carven roods,
with the words of the bug-eyed traveller
still ringing in our lug-holes, *Look out!*
We have all kinds of idiots round here,
someone was stabbed in Saltersgill last week,
we reached the subway tunnel
under the dual carriageway, the one
with the tendency to amplify, not only,
the sound of receding footsteps,
breath and the ancient glugging thread
of water that in giving itself away connects
rather than isolates each sore separation; so
who would've guessed April snowflakes
would be falling, like down, by the time
we emerged from the clot of darkness?

Sympathy for the Night

The wind, which has wailed through town
hysterical, rambling about a pandemic,
drops and the darkness seems to expand
in sound's absence, as if it squats to rest
from the buffeting, as if it has no
intention of shunting off anywhere soon.

And why would it?

Each day brands the night a vagrant,
shooing it away, kicking it on, clad in
hi-viz vests, helmets, steel capped boots,
with good-riddances and official writs
of 'Get thee gone' signed by the Sun;
but for now this night can stake out a plot,
unroll a groundsheet, trace constellations.

The Details Burn
(After Muhaned Durubi's The Waiting Nightmare*)*

Oh, that dream last night was so vivid,
there was, I'm sure, a bright lemon sky,
a blue hillside, the yellow shone on me
but fine details turn to ashen flakes.

There was, I think, a ripe lemon sky,
my headless body hung on a chemtrail
but fine details burn to ashen flakes,
I was alone, I know, apart from the dog.

My headless body swung on a chemtrail,
I lost fragments of self in the drying wind,
I was alone, I know, apart from the dog
and the air had such a submarine feel.

I lost fragments of self in the drying wind,
oh, last night's dream was just so vivid
and the air had such a submarine feel,
on the blue hill, such yellow shone on me.

Ei Mitään

One of us says *exuberance*,
points to fresh sparklings
at the tips of branches,
soft petals and catkins shaken
in the dance of a Spring day.

One of us whispers *inevitable*
like a slow-motion
explosion
that runs through everything
as microscopic bonding;
the marsh is giddy with gold.

One of us speaks *silence*
so that we might hear swan-glide,
the wing beats of *pica pica*,
Now then Jack, how's your brother?
flood waters from the river-spill
have eaten our way back.

One of us says *secret*
and out of it comes silhouette:
a young deer bounding
through our hair, along nerves
to their ends, leaping through
a blizzard of static electricity
quivering between trees.

To Charm the River

Toss a pebble so it skims
the ripples once, twice,
three times
before it drops
to sink to stir her
from her bed,
scatter grass and daisies
across brown eddies
where sunlight glistens
and when she turns
on a tidal shift
ask her politely
to come to tea.
Go home and wait
patiently for when
and if she arrives
you will recognise her
as your Great Aunt Peg
from your Nana's photos
wearing a swan feather bonnet
a weed green coat
a seal pelt shawl pinned
by a broach of jet, her breath
will be full of foxgloves.
She will flow
through the house
taking a path of least resistance,
under the surface of her skin
semi-translucent,
shifting like rain in puddles
are pot dogs on a window sill,

old nuts, washers, bolts, chains
from broken hoists,
from derailed trolleys.
Threatening to spill
beyond her edges she will settle
in a chair, sip her tea, nibble cake,
reminisce about her headlong rush
from Crossfell toward the Gares,
tumbling between eroded rocks,
the leap of High Force,
the turns and twists
through tangled woods,
the brush of boats,
the scrape of ships –
of fish and tadpoles,
dragonflies, a heron's beak,
a cloud of midges, the dip
and drip of a water wheel
and how once upon a while
folk would worship her
for the life and death
she brought before we thought
we'd tamed her seasonal swell.
Her voice will splash
and babble on, lap-lapping
against your consciousness
gently lulling you into sleep
and when you wake, she's gone,
having slipped away
leaving soppy footprints
across the kitchen floor.

Watching the Witch

I see you through the hole in the witch stone,
pale in the sun against a salmon wall,

framed by the green tangles of potted herbs,
your eyes squint slices of arctic twilight,

you flash a lopsided quizzical smile,
spells of silver flash from your pierced ears,

small flowers tattooed on your shoulder,
a bruise fading in the well of your inner arm,

your hand strokes a leaf like an old familiar,
a band of gold encircling one finger

like a cooled spark from the sun's corona,
you lean in, rest your head against my cheek,

your third eye opens its spiral staircase,
through the hag stone's hole our two souls meet.

The Handfasting

She calls to me
in the shadow of the bridge
with a voice laced with suds and whisky
and I see the wisdom of the world
inverted yet locked in the eye
of a mule as it bends the ridge of its spine
to drink from the roadside pool.

She calls to me
and I am bewildered by the slime-
coated rocks of the riverbank
in the shadow of the bridge,
the cloying stink of churning waste,
the deceptive lure of exposed silt beds
beneath the bridge blessed by floodlights.

She calls to me
in gilt, purpled, greened girders
against a torn veil of clouds, far flung
clusters of stars, rice someone's
scattered across the sky's black turf,
in the shadow of the bridge
I lob half a brick out into the flow.

As she calls to me
just to break solitude's hold
from the shadow of the bridge,
and the brick shatters the surface
with a ring of splinters, a wreath of ripples
to stop the reflections, for a moment
from thinking me, drinking me whole.

Second Quarter

"...and it's
spring

when the world is puddle-wonderful..."

EE CUMMINGS

Spell

When the half-moon gobbles up clouds,
compass the bees to keep them all calm,

they know the plot where you once buried
The Bad Times but they'll keep it a secret

if you sip a dewdrop, spit it into your palm
clench the fist tight then slowly unfold it

to feed the faie-wind's nuzzling mouth.

Life Lessons

Dad demonstrates
the right way
to catch a thrown house brick,
guiding it into a gloved cradling

almost like catching a baby.

Then he begins to hurl them
up to me on the scaffold;
we find a rhythm as his stack
diminishes

mine grows.

Once his has vanished
he'll clamber up the ladder and
I'll watch him build the world.

Message

From the raised promenade
I watch black clouds build
to the North, smothering
the Headland, the ships
queuing at Teesmouth,
the wind turbines, my home;
feel flecks of icy rain on my face,
but it's a bitter text on my phone
that causes me to shudder.

Shade

There it goes
bleak brother of absence,
    flitting, under-exposure
sliding over brickwork

keeping pace
with each stride, bulge bag
slung over its shoulder
full of tricks, snakes, gadgets
and top-secret files
a can of worms he's avoided opening.

Does he hold all the forgotten
moments of my life
in his expanding-shrinking flatness?

While my right argues with my left,
my consciousness slops
    spills
        leaks
through pin-holes in any premise,
flips faith like a coin –
not heads nor tails
    but both
when in mid-spin in the air at noon.

And when is it ever
not mid-spin
in the air at noon?

So, I stop and stare
    and ask
if his two dimensionality
without the depths of doubt
allows him to believe
unconditionally?

Or is he, familiar stalker,
forerunner,
        hanger-on, convinced
by his own practiced mimicry?

Triskelion

Today I am three
seagulls in the high spring wind,
one lagging behind the others,

struggling to keep up
on the whistling yowl that is melody
to the just-budding trees, pinpricks

of colour as infectious as funk and the thin
surprising sunlight idly tossing

a trio of shadows like empty bin bags
across King Edward's Square,

today there seems
little point to claim coalescence,
no sadness nor terror in this.

Today's Threads

From the industrialist's inside pocket
the navvies' descendants
        post the latest status updates
across the humming hive mind

and like a soothsayer's mumblings
        over entrails,
their skin-sloughing posts
are a dust storm of secular prayer

but on the ever-stream of my feed I find –
        more than trolls and counter trolls
reflecting clashing currents of public view –

seven *Óskmey* circling my chair
        savage angels above antennae
gliding, threading wind-paths through air.

Good Friday

Faint, at first, as a groan
        clenched between
teeth from a few millennia ago,
but enough
to stop you in your tracks, head
cocked and breathing stilled
for a moment as you listen
to the quiet it left behind, as if
the whole of the woodland
is stunned at the hearing;
        wind down the river
testing surface tensions
drops like a shroud
to sink among the reeds.

It comes again, a burst
        of rapid drilling, sheer
ferocity, silence bleeding
after its pricking,
beak penetrating the flesh
        of the holy rood
to snatch a shred of spirit
to sustain itself, sap leaking
from opened wounds,
        liquid gold, tacky
between thumb and index finger.

The Trail Back

There's a whole load of starting points,
random platforms of imminent departure,
like the tattered flag of a dusty cobweb
draught-dancing in the classroom corner
or at the back of the checkout queue
in Tesco Express or the crawl of a rush
hour tail back on a junction of the A1M

but from any one the veil can tear and run
to shunt you through leaving the 4-pack
of Stella Artois on the tiles, the cigarette
smoking in the ashtray, the chewed biro
dropped on the open page, and stripped
of uniform, tie, blazer or T-shirt and jeans,

and there's the primal forest, the sacred
oak, low brooding sky, wolf spoor, grim-
slick crows' feast, the animal hide wrapped
about your sinews, you realise you must
follow the deer tracks through the trees,
pad silent past barrows, squat in the thicket,
weigh the spear in your hand, listen for drums.

Big Sea

Nu sculon herigean heofonrices Weard,
Meotodes meahte ond his modgeþanc, – Cædmon's Hymn

What must I sing? said Cædmon.
Sing, he said, *about the beginning of created things.*

I'll sing of high spume and brisk winds,
the air studded with diamonds,

As enthralled, we watch these walls
of wild water leaping over the pier,

How they swallow each other,
rise again in ongoing resurrections.

When they reach for us with icy fingers
we burst with laughter that shatters

Like stage-glass about us, runs away
through shivering silver puddles;

What must I sing? said Cædmon.
Sing, he said, *about the beginning of created things.*

While a shag poses for photos
perched upon the sea defences,

Peering along the black length
of its beak, egging us on to sing

Snatches of Cædmon's holy verses
to the boom, slap and spit

Of the sea's orchestra, stretched
between Winter and Spring.

What must I sing? said Cædmon.
Sing, he said, *about the beginning of created things.*

Rose Tinted Rhapsody

The rose clouds are blooming
above these terraced streets,
petals uncurling like baby fingers
beckoning each earthbound thing
to unpeel and shed its casing, let go
and flow as evaporated scruples
to enter the anther, to dine upon
sun-dust and settle in their pistils,
for it is early Spring, the daylight
whetted and the air still thin,
with blasts of an old war film
seeping through brick and mortar
in waves from a neighbour's TV,
and me slithering across the ceiling.

Sunshine After the Shower

Holding itself together beneath still-warring
cloudscapes, the yard glows like a light bulb
flicked on and fizzing with an instantaneous
warmth, the leaves dazzle with drying jewels,
breeze-stirred upon freshly sanctified stalks.

From the white filament of the washing line
damp, wooden pegs hang amongst pearls,
a shoal taking respite from their downfall
while redirecting sharp beams of sunlight
towards newly re-calibrated destinations.

Shadows of indifferent seabirds stone-skim
across the grattage-puddled concrete floor
vanishing into vacant terracotta plant pots;
stacked babushkas beside a greening gate,
as bedraggled survivors begin to emerge

from hideaways in the nooks and crannies:
antennae, horns, hooflets, beaks, buttocks
test out the pristine alignments of wreckage,
rearrangements made by the weight of rain,
resuming once again their busy proliferation.

The brightness dims as cloudscapes churn,
a blue bottle hammers at the window pane
to shatter transparency with a targeted drone,
vapours rise like smoke signals after a strike,
our theme tune fades in, the end credits roll.

A Tub of Nostalgia

The moon-scooped roof of the old A.B.C. Picturehouse
is an abandoned flying saucer from a 1950s B Movie
with its thinly veiled analogies to the last Cold War,

the terror from the skies, the screams of doomed extras,
the necessary threat an alien invasion produces
for the construction and maintenance of collective identity,

and the lobster red
brick walls are anchored by an exoskeleton of scaffolding,
doors shuttered fast and the upper rows of seats inside

thick with a silence that is nothing to do
with expectancy or suspense,
or the anticipated sweetness of ice cream on a wooden stick

nor the quiet between beats in the years it functioned as a night
    club,
but the light from the dismantled projector still cuts the air
heavy with the smell of hotdogs, spilt beer, popcorn, sawdust,
    petting

and the impregnated dreams
of so many generations, the endless
prairies, greased lightning, deep blue, monster as familiar,

the Aston Martin burning rubber on a mountain track, the man
capable and willing to spin the Earth backwards, the loss
that drives you to the edge, and over it, once you reach

the loose end of the reel suddenly to realise
all those pictures on the wall have stopped their flickering
and the movie still playing is the one

in your head's long corridor as you navigate the crossroads
in Spring sunshine, you and your shadow self,
stepping together, toward me, in tune to the green man's beep.

Tai Qi Among the Crows

My single whip latches the trunks of trees
that cast a drooping canopy of hefty green
over the latticework of paths between mounds,
softly pregnant pillows of grass, a dream
interred with other dreams seeding the ground.
The crows spook the buttercup-lawns with keys
to unlock ancestral avenues tucked under wing
or kept in breast pockets of funereal coats
as I rotate my axis and repulse the monkey,
these corbies joggle like puppets on strings
before one rises, claiming to be the King of Ghosts,
floats upon a warm airwave to the mariner's grave,
caws with nonchalance from the stone anchor,
and eyes my green dragon emerging from water.

Caught in the DC Multiverse

It wasn't the lack of comedy that led me to detect
that all was not as it seemed in the world of captions,
speech bubbles, those block-printed sound effects
as I slipped between the irregular frames of each
graphically inked instant of dramatic action, where no
one ever watched the garden whilst sipping a glass
of lemonade without it being laced with deadly poison
or gamma radiation or without the peaceful summer
scene being shattered by the imminent invasion of a
psychopathic alien in a skin-tight costume of primary
colours whose destiny was to consume all worlds
and the lemonade drinking garden-watcher was none
other than our all-time favourite cosmic, battle
seasoned, saviour cunningly disguised as common
or garden Joe Shmo to lure the planet-devouring
super-villain into a false sense of security, to land him
'Slap-Bang' in the trap of advanced science from which,
eventually, he'll manage to escape and flee, tail tucked
between his legs, but vowing revenge and promising
to return by issue #156; leaving me to misinterpret
every mundane occurrence as the lead-in to some
apocalyptic struggle between Good and Evil, all for
the sake of a scarred soul but held secure behind
its vigilante mask of justice and sacrifice; while
sitting on the corrugated garage roof we'd talk in half
worried tones about all those big questions like how
many sit-ups it would take to build a six pack like
Superman's, how practical was the length of Batman's
cape and what in the multiverse were we supposed
to do to start growing pubic hair, down there.

Film

The day is shrink wrapped in cellophane

    I weigh it in my hands
and peer through the protective sheen

at the buildings, trees, concertinaed roads,
the folds of weather and the people

    some I recognise, some I don't.

    If I prick my ears I can just
make out the tidal wash of their muted

conversations tightly packed
and impenetrable.

Like so many plastic packets
my clumsy fingers can't split the seam

    to scatter the treasures

across the floor and sort them into
new arrangements, instead I carry it

    around like a birthday cake
then take a nap and use it as a pillow.

Hand and Arm
(After a Photograph by Kev Howard)

    ...like the Buddha's
a whole universe rests in this palm

floating in empty space

in a spiral of procrastination
    ...scum circling a plug hole

expecting something to happen
a spark maybe......a long continuous

B   A   N   G

infinite expansion

into an ink stain
    a Rorschach blot

where ghosts dance and sing
    stars explode
ice caps form and melt

and the drowning man
transforms, evolves, becomes

shadow to show how we
might become beings of light –

as a shadow cannot but point to light
as a martyr dies so we might live

in understanding of sacrifice – oh,
    ...a dark wisdom this!
        which he asks us to bear

reconfiguring consciousness
through a surgery of the psyche

to resist the obvious shaping
to form ourselves anew.

Curved Form (Delphi)
(After Barbara Hepworth)

Note the hollow
  String the egg
    Yolk the flesh
      Stone the embryo
        Preserve the peel
        Slice the pulp
          Bite the curve
            Swallow the seed
            Core the stone
              Strum the yolk
                Sound the nut
              Spit the pip
                Peel the skin
                  Split the sound
                    Swallow the white
                  Stone the strum
                Draw the shell
              Sex the fruit
              Pluck the apple
            Polish the nut
            Seed the core
            Dunk the promise
          Dowse the body
        Flesh the curve
        Pierce the skin
      Shell the bite
      Pulp the echo
      Tell the tale
    Curve the chord
  Hollow the note

Kirkcarrion

The warblings of wary ewes
watching us through slitted stares

from terraces of slate,
riddled with boltholes
to hidden warrens that run
to the hill's stilled core,

a winding, cropped-grass scar
across the grizzled god's upper lip
gouged cheeks and brow
up to the crown of Scotch Pine

behind a fleece-rubbed dry-stone wall,
where rabbit vanishes through a gap
too small to follow, so we climb,

careful, over snug, well-placed rocks
to drop onto lush grass, well-held shade,
enclosed shelter with a cairn-child
marking the centre,

the moon rests here to sip its milk,
dribble light into Lune and Tees,
we tread circles of faith to view
the settlement's rough bark, leathers,

furs and bronze, patient tokens
lost to the barrow, Prince Rabbit
on the Ram's Horn Throne perched

as if he's carved from sandstone,
tunnel-bound beneath our toes,
hoarding centuries in each bulb's eye

like he's dreamed us here
to scaffold his edges,
to haul the whole
of his depth from darkness.

Beyond the Flesh
(After David Watson)

A dozen disembodied faces – disciples
mourning an extinguished flame like those
I glimpse sometimes behind closed lids,
body relaxed, sleep flooding the bedroom –
the rising water level sloshing
around the bed, lifting it, sweeping it away
like a raft adrift upon night tides.
The faces are clouds in a smoggy sky
where the moon has bled out.
Those faces are bubbles rising
in the ocean my bed-raft rides upon,
popping as they break the surface, each
releasing a syllable of song sung in the natural
acapella of pain fermented from primal soup.

The Jig of Light
(After Tony Charles)

As if on a mission to find whatever it was
someone once brushed under the carpet,
he is stripping layers through abrasion,
the grinder's pressure, angle and sweep
is a speed-boat fettling waves, its rudder
scoring out jazz lines, swirls and squiggles
in an effort of undoing, sweat on his cheek,
distorting fake signage to frame a partial
obtuse question in this ritual scratching
of the looking glass's hard, unblinking face –
as if an answer might come from scribbling
sigils in damp sand with a driftwood stick,
the high tide rushing in over itself, roaring
through his ears, hammer, anvil, stirrup,
to swallow all spellings, to tow away all
signage and to leave him lost and baffled
'unpainted', suspended, just out of reach.

Those Tubes that Bore Messages

We bumped into Aunt Enid outside
Tower House, that became Debenhams,
when it had those tubes they used
to shoot the sales orders between
different departments and floors.
My parents were full of concern,
I guessed something very sad
had happened, maybe someone
had died, didn't Mam say something
the other day about poor Uncle Ted
when I was reading Spider-Man?
Anyway, what I remember now
was Enid's response to some question
of how she was holding up,
I'll get through it, I have to...
But I'm ready to go and I never
want to do this again. The shop
mannequins were watching,
the shoppers streamed around us.
I don't remember much more
than those words cascading
onto the pavement around our feet
like shards of glass from a brick
lobbed through Binns' windows,
how, with all of this wild life
surging within us, anyone would tire
of playing with it, trying to shape it,
riding its wave to its crest, what
I didn't know then was the cost
of loving, the strain it takes
to stand in the shallows and smile
while exchanging some familiar
well-meant pleasantries
when your world has imploded.

Tincture

The chimney is snoring
                    as she sleeps,
I sit by the window
having paced
around the house like a blind man,
        fingertips
brushing the walls,
the crenelated edges
of inherited cabinets,
                the spines
of dusty books,
sent the globe on a single spin
to let April's sunlight
                    splash
across The Middle Kingdom
as if to test today's solidity,
                or my own
as if I am
inhabiting her slumberlands
        of slow recovery
wading through a maze
of memories
within her brain's posterior cortical.

There is a theory
    that water has memory,
has the ability to retain
the residual information
                of the things
it has absorbed
come into contact with
    inhabited   experienced
merged with in a process
    of molecular union.

The walls of this house
                       pulse
in the early afternoon sunlight,
appear translucent
                like a blister;
the living room
is filling with fluids
                pouring from a tap
in the parietal lobe,
                  it sounds
like the ringing
            of a phone
to the emergency services,
                it sounds
like rising panic
                it sounds
like a lesson in patience
no need, now, to hold
my breath   close my eyes
to the flood.
Will these soul-waters
    remember me
when next she wakes?

Witchtide

This time last year you were in hospital
with breast cancer, the year before that
it was still touch and go with your brain
haemorrhage – whether or not
the surgery would prove successful;
but look at us sitting together today,
you prodding me in the ribs with a stick
out of mischief to see how far you can
push it and me trying to read Laurie Lee
stepping out one morning into a world
neither of us would recognize, I'm
trying to take it all in, this whole
dreaming in a gathering of awareness:
how I'm dazzled by the glimmer
of Spring sunlight on the lazy river,
how my eyes are lured by the hazy
blanket over the land's crooked spine,
how I'm mesmerized by the drips
from the dipping beak of a swan, let loose
by the metronome slice of a paddle,
captivated by that black log's clockwise
rotations in the current, surprised
by the leap and belly-flop of a frog,
drawn toward a campfire's smoke trails
in the woods, how I'm fixated on counting
the railings in the reflection of the bridge,
curious to know how long the black coot
will stay submerged, how we're led
astray by tyre tracks and hoof prints
pressed into the mud, how I'm snagged
by the water hag's lip as she slips
between early blossom trees in rags
collecting washed up odds and ends;
fragmentary trophies like me, like you.

Third Quarter

"A something in a summer's noon –
A depth – an Azure – a perfume –
Transcending ecstasy."

EMILY DICKINSON

Beltane

We have come away, we three,
from the sprawl to where we might,
by chance, bump into ourselves
on a certain chore, half nod in recognition
and hurry back through some expectant door;

we have come away to taste a little time
between our deadlines and demands
parking fines and career plans
to pitch a tent and coax a fire
to watch a crow watch us
from the perch of a telephone wire,

to seep into a sea of seed drifts
dusting the grass with blossom;
the early dazzle stuffed with airborne fluff
the breeze likes to kick into tiny wylms –
stray ideas, unmoored half-thoughts
in piebald deer-shade; a time of licking flames,

of shooting sparks, soot, steam, oil stains,
of vintage trains hooting through a tunnel,
of sea-coal stories burning in the firebox;
a time to draw the thread of strength
from ancestors who have passed along the track
for they too knew difficult days and nights

that begat grief and guilt in a world
of blood and greed and born-bred duty
of 'know thy place,' but watched, like we do,
as Summer's face grew in the bark of trees,
blinking stones on the river bed; in a time
of dancing swifts above the farmhouse eaves,

smudges of maiden pink poking from behind
the hedge; that other wind – it comes in waves
down this green dale, a stream of moments,
wing beats, wafts of wild garlic, stroking
everything it passes, dipping branches,
scuffing mole hills that mark the under-life

in soil beneath the restless hooves of calves,
bearing the world away from yesterday,
untying tomorrow with all its duty-borne demands,
flung like confetti and the fairy fur of dandelion clocks
that carries us, three clowns, away like down.

Chaffinch Among the Daffodils

And later as the dusk drifted in,
as we flicked switches on lamps,
drew curtains on the street, I heard
again, the scales, the winding stream
practiced upon its hoarded rocks,
the flow notes, trills, arpeggios
that sent a shiver down my spine,
and saw once more the daffodils
brightening the banks of Farndale
between trees with buds clamped,
felt the flit and dart of a chaffinch
in my ribcage, singing a golden song
striking notes that sent sap rising,
as we strolled along to Low Mill.

Abracadabra

like a music hall magician
the sun steps out
from behind curtains of clouds
and we all glance up,

everyone tilts their faces
skyward

to feel its presence
tickle their cheeks;

it speaks through touch,
a fizz on the skin of all things solid
but it is only the liquids
that readily commit to its beckoning.

Come, it says, *lift and rise, rise and drift.*
and all that's wet obeys:

the raindrops on leaves
the puddles in the road
the blood in my veins

particle by particle
dance, lift, rise and drift

like party balloons
like bubbles in a pan on the hob
like applause to the end notes
of an ancient song.

The old cow shed

lost its doors an age ago, gable
bearded, eves browed with ivy,
the corrugated salmon flesh
of its sagging roof – an occasional
perch for scrutinising crows.
The murk within is thickened
by two shafts of sunlight
from missing tiles; swallows
dart in and up to their nest
among the rafters. In one corner
lies a rust-pitted hammer –
the shaft snapped, a beaten stone,
an abandoned stirrup, and it hasn't
shaded a cow's hide in years. Instead
it listens for the lap of the Esk,
the crunch of footsteps on the toll track
to Egton, the hooves' daily plod
of its outgrown herd on the path
to and from the milking yard; suckling
shadow, swallows, creeping ivy,
the quivering heads of cow parsley.

Sheepwash

Squatting on tumbled sandstone boulders
in the middle of the brook's babble
of bass lines, treble beats, djembe finger pats,
of liquid on the move, running with the breeze
that bends the pinked seed-heads of grasses,
ruffles the pelt of a bee roaming purple
thistle crowns, I wonder what it's saying.

A grass sprite with antennae lands
on my forearm, the lightest of tickles,
as if testing the solidity of alien ground,
though it knows the water's song –
does it know that Mam brought me and John
here on Summer holidays to play in the stream,
while she sunbathed with a book?

The brook's babble is constant
though we don't hear it all the time
as consciousness sifts perceptions,
memories:

same rocks
same water
same wind
same little bridge.

My daughter lies on the clover bank,
quietly absorbed in her book.

It's like Time stands still
and it's us that run through it
like ghosts through ground mist.

The Nine Sisters

The paths not only twist but shift,
bog shluck, tree tremble, grinding
a pancrack sky against worn rock,
walk the perplexity of circles as if
in the Nave of Chartres Cathedral,
by fern bed, nettle dossal, mallow,
blackberries; a pebble dropped
into a hidden well plummeting
through darkling years, torpid air,
this hillside's gullet, and the Nine
stay cloistered somewhere within
greenery gossiping in stone tongues,
bird stains, unearthed flint points,
of promised peels of thunder
that make your neck hairs bristle.
Best to turn back toward the car
abandoned by the five-bar gate
into a field of puddled furrows, but
don't look back at Spring Heeled Jack
tearing, hare-like, along the hedgeline.

Everything Under the Sun
*"Like a thief I crept and entered a house,
And it was my own home!"* – Rumi

The wave's lip
   stammers
  sips dry sand
kisses your toes
    swings back
beneath the wings
       of sandpipers

The next gathers
its gift of dark distance
     in a French fold
that   breaks   apart
   on the sandbank

It is a breathing
     machine
  and   sometimes
it's the quiet   voice
that penetrates the din
  to enter the brain

Imagine the angel
(the best possible you)
  terribly unleashed
from the tightrope
 of survival
with fuck all to lose
       or gain

Try counting the swells
and your numbers
      will sink to roll
  rub and grind
away their edges
     as sand grains

realising the innumerable
you

  on dry land
you
   the gathering swell
you
  the synchronised flock
of sandpipers
you
   the wind
     in their feathers
the vast breathing
machine
the balanced wave
you
   the crash   the bubble
the sound of the first number
held in the curl
      of a breaker

Splendere

    this   air   sparkles
    each   sea-wrinkle
    is etched   momentarily
    into the strange reality
    of uncalendared   days
    I fall   into the clarity
    of each sand grain's
        glisten   our shadows
            move   toward
    the wavelet's final   reach
    watch its shy shrink back
         in bubbles
    under   a flock of knots
    that settle
    like surf-rounded pebbles
        where it stroked
        the land
    this side of the mark
        where oystercatchers
    wade   bright bills poised
    to prick
    the membrane
          of sky
    reflected in each singular ripple
    pierce
        the passing lightness

The Birthing

There is never a full rehearsal for this,
one thing I recall is the sound of gulls
wheeling outside like spectres in mist.

The world with its singular woe and bliss –
a cargo transported in ghost ships' hulls,
there's no adequate rehearsal for this.

So, I stroked her back. I planted a kiss
in waves of pain that sharpens then dulls,
swells and shrinks like outside in the mist

raptors or angels fresh from an abyss,
their cries blossom within our skulls,
There can be no rehearsals for this!

Stranded at a beginning I can't dismiss
where raw existence shoves and pulls
to wheel outside like phantoms in mist.

The details won't fit as we try to reminisce,
China trodden under the hooves of bulls,
there is never a dress rehearsal for this;
are we still wheeling, waiting in the mist?

Creation Myth

I was birthed by the Boiling River,
spewed like froth onto tidal mud
amongst shredded tyres, plastic bags
and rust-bitten scraps of broken things.

I wailed my liquid longing
into the midsummer night,
a strawberry moon stared out
its submerged twin, mouthful
of spearwort and horsetail.

The river witch, Peg, well – she
was sleeping off the labour
dreaming scales, skeletons, hunger.

The strawberry moon scooped me up,
suckled me on sour milk and Litha's fruit
then set me loose to lope
through humanity's creases.

Noctilucent Clouds

When you've become nothing but silhouette,
stark against the tidal glow of Paddy's Hole,

when the coal inside's lost hold of its smoulder
to the pinpricks of lamps beyond the mouth

and even the salted weeds have turned dumb
to your blather or your half-hearted excuses,

when you're thinned out by desire, look up;
materialising as strands of airborne cobweb

silver blue embroidery of the high night sky
still catching the beams of light from a sun

that's sunk beneath the sea's darkened rim,
the signatures of midsummer sprites who flit

across the mesosphere in a jig of secret joy,
folding space into the shapes of possibilities

creasing flexigons from today and tomorrow,
too high, too faint, to view in daylight hours

these fine threads are plucked from dreams
of sleepers drowsing heavy in their beds,

unspooled from our cranium wells, towed
toward heaven to hang the ghosts of fireflies.

Tat Tvam Asi

The something about those long car journeys
after the fluster of departure and we'd settled
into the route and a comfortable quietude
and I could look out of the window at a tree
in a field with its shadow, the line of a hillside,
the folds of the moors under the raw clouds,
a greened boulder in the swell of heather
though the seeing was more like the tasting
of a fresh nettle leaf complete with its sting,
an ingesting that tugged me out of the car, out
of the body of the boy I was and into the thing
that was held within its solid, particular wonder
as if the Radio DJ had begun to chant *This Art
Thou* as we passed on our way to somewhere.

Watching Swallows at Ludworth Tower

To sweep carefree the summer thermals
as those swallows flitting high, scything low,
feathering unwired acrobatics
in a carnival of airborne control –
bone-chaff, flung upon the blast with a will
that hatched eager to ride it, unroll the length
of a draught and caress its living weave,
and so quick to learn the tailor's flair
to slice and scissor, then repair
the puncture holes where insects were
with a stitching beak and tail-wind braid
embroidering flight-paths
in the weft of pollen-drowsy air
that moves like a tide in today's
cloudless sky above my grounded head;
while inside my skull half-thoughts fly
too swift to snare with words,
but dart and dodge like fleeting birds
my tardy mind and lagging eye
too lumbering to track and trace,
from a spike foundered on the grass;
birds and insight evade the chase
as sand runs through an hourglass.

Feral, flipping consciousness, hopping
between eddies of heat-filled air;
it's show-time over scattered boulders
once a ceiling and the spiralling stair

of a Tower fortified against the Scots,
one wall remains with two windows
where sentries stood keeping watch
for signs of reivers, the smoke of gunshots,
their ears peeled for the dreaded beat
of iron-shod hooves, pipes and drums.

Lying among wildflowers like a fallen log,
I hear the distant bark of a farm's guard dog
come rolling, rootless, down the length of the dell
stirring sprigs of cow parsley, clumps of bluebell,
I train my focus on the salt-stained stones
that jut like a dragon skull's broken horns,
its hoard ransacked, its spilt secrets unknown
seeping, over centuries, through the topsoil.

This hillock ruin wears a gargoyle's grin
caught midway between laughter and despair,
as if wherever one ends the other will begin
like the undulations of ridge and furrow
that ghost-mark the field across the way,
flecked with dark spots of restless crows
lost to their dull, grating squabbles,
reaffirming bloodlines and hierarchies
only they would know and acknowledge.

Subdued colours blossom behind closed lids,
flickering faces from last night's dreaming:
an interrogation for an unspoken crime
in a dark cell that soaked up denial
for all the things that can't be named,
then set adrift at midnight on a fretful sea

to sink beneath waves of guilt and shame
where orcas tear into my fears and worries,
toss them around like bloodied seals
as I float among sunken masts and keels.

When I open my eyes, the swallows are back,
performing aerial displays of gymnastic tricks,
I try to follow the flick-dip-climb and tack
of their erratic, criss-crossing air-tracks
and feel a surge of inner grace
as last night's dream dissipates
replaced by nothing but an empty space
that rings like a Tibetan singing bowl,
its note splitting and rebounding
from every quarter of the soul.

The dancing passerines sew up heaven's coat,
warm-bodied needles with darkling wings,
a flash of pale breast, a blood red throat,
their tails form Vs for vector, or for victories,
feasting in a dizzying fit, mid-flight,
oh, the sheer majestic joy of it!
Fattening up with each sun-plump day
for an impending migration once Autumn calls,
then away, away, across oceans and deserts,
over rugged snowbound mountain summits,
through fog, storm clouds and gales, steering
a route by reading Earth's magnetic fields.

Misprediction

A few cool raindrops
is all that fell,

no thunder storms
to snap the leaden air,

still nodding
at the far end of the yard

a bright pair of poppies
lure a solitary bee,

although I have
swallowed last night's

lateness I'm parched
for the taste of sleep.

Hide and Seek

Walking away from thunder
by our side the black river's
placid slither, polished jet,
tell-tale bubbles, ring ripples,
light raindrops – cool kisses.

Electric blue rumblings,
you stroll through red poppies
in the muggy pre-storm heat.
You are a bright ladybird
resting on a willow leaf.

I'm a handful of grass seeds
stripped off a blade you scatter
among nettles by the path,
the storm horses are snorting,
stamping hooves upon farm roofs.

A Police helicopter,
like a damsel fly, patrols
charged skies and reflections,
hunting for missing persons
borne along by undercurrents.

Horseshoe Bend, Thornaby

A small peninsula
    ploughed
        by a river's
oxbow meander,
a trail through wet grasses,
    high reeds
and woodland, and
after distraction, exercising
    a right to roam
froglets
the size of a fingernail
   scamper   underfoot,
the lure of willy-nilly
    rings scattered
on slow waters,
I could swim its breadth,
    I'm sure of it –
the spit or kiss of clouds,
spots of blackened charcoal
    ash smudges
from the secret life of fires
I'd have loved to light,
    that danced
their brief flickerings
    across inky ripples
toward a sunken moon,
    and who
wouldn't wade into the still

green pool of metamorphosis –
    a liquid heart
that hides pre-industrial toilings,
    shards of pottery,
a rust-bitten blade, fishbones,
a prayer to Minerva
bubbling up through centuries
    of silt,
layers of decay;
sitting on sandstone blocks
    we watch
the steady flow,
the estates of Thornaby and Stockton
    bustle on behind veils
of mirrored trees
    each side
of the water-snake-wynd,
    we're trying
to read the currents
as we've done for thirty years
    or more
and I imagine
    generations of eyes
towed gently downstream.

Border Blessing

Just for a moment, let's stop here,
having set an automatic reply on Outlook,
shot off out of reach to a quiet spot
not known of before to sit in the shade
of a young rowan, its leaves serrated,
quivering tears; eyes surveying the slopes
of Ruberslaw without any immediate
threat of reiving moss-troopers, as the sky
deepens into ponderings that pluck,
from nowhere, a pinked half-moon
marbled with mould, while the whoop
of wood pigeons sends it buoying higher
it is the crows' caws that cut it loose.

Let's wake next morning glen-swaddled
in a blanket of mist that has swallowed
all directions and distances; the wooden
slats of the shepherd's hut, each blade
of grass, thistle heads and holly bushes
tethered together by dew-heavy cobweb.

Dunbar Dream-Song

By Broxmouth Woods
my dreams come in droves:
of gull-spume and spray veils
at the tide mark of Bass Rock,
of ragged lines of dun geese
singing farewell to the quarry,
the warble of crumbling ruins,
kittiwake shrieks and sea pinks
and toadstool gills by the burn,
of ghost-bairns racing barefoot
through thickets, dangling
from branches, raiding nests
for mottled treats to ward off
a stitch or pangs of hunger,
of failures known, shrugged off,
unrecognised, old infidelities
picked clean as sea-winds flap
at our tent, tug the guide-ropes,
shake the poles and pegs,
of a silver thumbprint smudged
in a tarnished sky over a cement-
works chimney, of troopers
preparing to strike at first light,
the subsequent scramble, screams,
slaughter, flight from the reeking,
the capture of colours
and blue cap surrender,
the harrowing march to the South,

of soft-grey thistle heads quivering
at dawn, seed-drift over
a golden meadow just this side
of the Summerlands, the ever-
shifting shades of the treeline,
of storm clouds sweeping in
from the Kingdom of Fife;
by Broxmouth Woods
my dreams come in droves.

Old Uncle Tay

The loch's blessing is its sleight-of-hand swell
palmed by a pre-nup' of giants, one dolled up

as cloud, another in needles, thistle, bracken,
a third a gasp when the sun blushes her jaw,

another in nothing but stoic patience; its
relentless slap 'n' tickle at all the wholesome

broken bits with its so many numb mouths
slurping the humbugs of quartz, barite, flint,

honey root, wolf stone, hermit's prayer –
as well as the reasons for his seclusion;

their erosion into each season's amnesia is a
savouring of drift-branches down to milk stains,

vanishing tricks, then finding a brand new
penny behind each of our left ears, a wink

to beg forgiveness for its compulsive borrowing
and gifting back, transformed. Just like that…

Measurements
(In Ullapool)

You lap the salt of Loch Broom
from wet fingers. It tastes like
the last place on Earth.

All the mountains
you've passed today still
thunder through your mind

like dominoes click-
clacking on the tabletop,
gulls squabbling over scraps.

As daylight swims out
toward the Summer Isles
and the dark crawls down

from the corries, you calibrate
the properties of memories
of all your favourite places;

your instruments:
a finger of driftwood from the shore,
a flat white stone from a Pictish fort.

Water Feature Beside the Bottle of Notes

The pigeons are mooching around the central pond
the tiddlers flick and twitch beneath the ripples

In one eye of the boys, who is young enough to hold
all desire in his eye, the tiddlers are crying to be caught

The pigeons eye the boys as they gather on the bank
with nets, a black bucket and an empty jam jar

The tiddlers weave secret trails through the reeds
their liquid calls fill the boy's ear, themselves

Small fry slipping through the labyrinth of canals
riding the feather-soft purr of pigeons busy pecking

Gregg's pasty crumbs dropped on the pavement
the bare topped boy fills the bucket with pond water

Sinks his own face, white pebble, into its depths,
becomes a small pale fish caught up in a ripple

A spit, a splash, the dip of a net into his liquid cries
the bob of a pigeon's head to the beat in his breast.

Dog-Day

Late July, midday, in the wide, flat, fallow field
                                            only I cast shade
the scrub is brittle,
        the ground crumbles under dusty feet,

we carry the sun's heat-litter upon our shoulders,
                                      drunk on its flames,
it feeds us   with flares,
we fan it with black feathers, our wingtips are singed,
there is sod-all   else
but distances receding along thorn-sprung hedgerows
unreachable as the ghost-light of dearly departed stars
                                  in the self-effacement
of teenage idolatries   –   who was it
you desperately wanted to be?   rig and furrow
                                        are waves of toil –
monuments to whatever's left of labour, the grindstone
                                    sky refuses to hold

any notion of cloud,
it's drained the matinée film of dew through a discarded

straw
                                       with a half-life
of two hundred years, it is greedy for names,
                                and now who
among us can recall what the Holy Maid was called?
        thing   -   ummy- bob
                       –   thunder-mountain

stuff my beak with wool, our old nest is a dust bowl, both
air and stone flow   and melt
as waves at the edge of an ocean, the rainbow spray
                                        is hysterical
a freakish millennial –
shrill tongue torn from her mouth, each finger set in a splint,
                                    didn't you see
the big wigs' bile at her divine revelations – proper
                                    lost their shit
when she prophesized how we would soon lose this kingdom:
                                    malicious revelations
                                    overflowing
with deniable data because everything is dismissible,
dryness of your mouth   –   suck on a pebble
keep weaving the mirage of fairy tale endings, sweet happy-
                                    ever-afters
for prepped survivalists   –   my shadow beetles
                                    for the trees,
snake rattle, blistering winds, where leaves store time
                                    for one season
only out on the flat, fallow field there's no longer a future
                                    for fixed
                                    raggy-arsed

   scarecrows.

Rift Woods

Waves of leaves
on a warm breath
a half-hidden footbridge
to the other side
burn babblings
the grinding call of the sea
entangled branches
waves of leaves
gravel pathways
the severed stump
refusing death
new growth. Moss
light splashes light drips
waves on a warm breath
greens wash my thoughts away
what's left?
Just eyes just ears
just skin.

Re-Wilding

Humidity   the air thickened with corn starch
and the undergrowth rampant
with sticky buds   bindweed's delicate white cones
bramble thorns and blood-red raspberries
        hanging in the tangles   as nettles
reach to brush passing ankles or stroke
your wrist with the lust of a long-lost lover   and everything
I've tried to achieve today   has been a non-starter,
the quiet in the house lead-weighted   drowning
each thought like a kitten tied in a bag of half-bricks
and flung from the bridge
                          into the tidal tow;
I've been all knees and elbows   beside myself
since waking, each time I try to fit into my skin
something bumps me out   as if
to say,
      You're not this adult creature confined
            to prescribed usefulness.
                   Have you forgotten
                          how useless you can be?

So long to worthy notions of productivity
                          of being handy
as a man should aspire to be and weigh his contributions
on the rigged scales of conscience   my mind
    it feels like mush   we're all expecting
a storm to break the heft, relieve the heat and restlessness
so I'm out exploring wastelands on a mountain bike
best to be off the well-worn tracks,
                        following abandoned routes
    round the back of facades, between named places
I'm sniffing about the skeletons of defunct industries
tumble-down offices   the remains of Ironopolis

                    liminal spaces
comforted by the swaddling nursery rhymes of grass and vine,
        There, there my lovelies,
                let's smooth off
                        those hard-man-made edges,
                                we'll find a new use for you yet.

All around me   cloisters
                of trees where Summer
has singed their edges and wallows
like suds and sludge on the surface of the becks
        that feed the river's pollen-dusted prayer house
                                of perpetual dusk
with the clapping of wood pigeon's wings, the strained eye
hovering in the air and keen ear a-tuned to unlikely
tell-tale rustles
amongst the mansions of moss and fungi;
                        I am forever
peering into the gloom for smaller ways still -
        half-trails that lead out of sight
toward unearthed alters   to sacraments
of sap and soil.   I obsess
over methods of abdication while positioning
        fallen branches, weaving twigs and sticks
to form nest or dray within which to dwell
        hidden and at arm's length away
from my usefulness   the greens stain
my hands and the seat of my pants
        splayed out on the dirt   staring up
through the thatch and layers of leaves
            at slivers of shifting light
it is so hard   to get back on the bike,
hard not to promise the rotting bark and mulch
        that I'll ever more lie here like this.

Holding Liquid

My long liquid memory net
       of the moon's elk wraiths

clings like restless sighing shadows
       of Baltic August back woods,

laid out as lake itself;
       reflection in a working cause

beyond this slide island's final full gaze,
       grips known effects, holds

bridge sounds of sail boats
       on reed waters, imprinting

tight correspondences
       to summer's shallows,

infinite masts sea cradle,
       archipelago beds spread

through life, tree sibling-
       tarot outcomes.

Gorge Tide

The rock flows in a white stream,
tumbles in torrents at a pace
beyond my mind's imagining.

The cavern echoes with drips
that carry the seeds of mountains,
grow slow geysers from still pools

that quenched the final thirst
of a man clad in wolf-hide
before his crow-soul flew free.

How far has the stone river run
since his last sip and this fingertip
wetting my lips from the same source?

All beyond the limestone chambers
flicker out but within we're preserved,
our very heart beats become calcified.

At Odds

When there's no hope of a phone signal
and I know, if there was, you wouldn't pick up
these are the things I can use to call you:
the mat of moss sighing damp over a tumble of rocks
among an oak's exposed roots beneath dripping branches,
the wind, carrying threads of fret into a white sky,
a distant dog's clockwork bark, pin pricks of sheep
on the farthest field, the infinite trembling pleats of the loch
running against itself, a low skein of geese, a fallen leaf
caught in the rhythm of a hidden waterfall, all packaged
into an irresistible lure bound to bring your voice to my ear,
your shadow striding from a copse of mountain ash,
shame berries crushed beneath bare feet
and my own dumb tongue hog-tied with string.

The Man in The Moon

Drawing the moon in its midway phase,
edging toward its final quarter, with all
of the intricacies of pockmarks, craters
thumb-stains, blemishes, mare prints:

Nectaris   Crisium   Tranquilitatis

I saw, in the countenance emerging from
6B scribbles, the patience of an ancient
gardener, like Ted's from the allotment
by Middlebeck with his miles-away stare

except when he looked at the living soil,
one who tended the dirt, knows full-well
he is originally of the earth, grown out of it
but standing apart in aching separation.

How it once coalesced from the shards
of impact and impregnation to hang
in a moth-like flutter around the flame
of its own making, suspended, watching

in a state of longing to cling to the gravity
of its parent, inheritance, tradition, with
its dark side simmering in the desire
to break free, a repulsion of recognition,

a will to become its own being, but how it
keeps these yin yang drives in balance
upon the scales of night-times, forever
swelling, shrinking through its germination.

Tarnished mirror for our own projections;
like the helplessness of knowing Dad has
taken ill, out of reach in Spanish hands,
we rely for knowledge on refracted light.

How Ted would finger the soil and know
there was a blight, reading how the particles
suffered from a case of collective dementia
and it's up to him to coax it back to memory.

Kite Over Morton Castle

Swallows are reaping harvests of midges
and water boatmen from the loch's hide,
scudding disturbances, breaking mirror
images of trees on the cusp, the jutting,
gnarled stone of the ruin standing roofless,
hollowed out, its seat of power long sunk,
swallowed up by sod while a red kite circles
effortlessly sailing air streams of this end-
of-August evening, scouring the scrub
for any sign of supper, its largo waltz
about the sky's ballroom, over the great hall,
the high-pitched whistle resounds off hillsides,
rings inside abandoned sheep skulls,
carries, like bloodlines, across centuries.

Pareidolia

Chimneypots, where the ragged sheets of clouds
flick by like pages of a musty encyclopaedia
given to you as an inquisitive child by a great aunt
whose papery skin would tear under the fingers
of her carers, whose voice was the soft crackle
of a needle on vinyl before the first note of a song;
her accent dense as a lump of Durham coal.

The clouds as they sail are hoarding light,
silent as owl wings, uncomplaining,
migrating at the will of a summer-sprung wind
over chimneypots that remind me of fingers
following lines of printed words,
determined to extract the wonders
of already outdated knowledge
from between embossed blue covers.

The mind returns to childhood, to rusty anchorings,
when whatever we read in the drifting shoals
of clouds was more than the promise of rain,
when rockpool crabs were armoured friends,
when the wispy voice of an ancient aunt
ploughed new furrows in an impressionable plot –
                                                forever
unspooling the start of a story of Uncle Jack,
of Esma, of Hilda, of Lorna, of Christopher;
all together again in the Empire of the Past
but which would always wind down
with the shortness of breath, the glass fish
watching from the windowsill illuminated
by the afternoon's sunlight swilling
like a flood tide through the rose garden.

When I look again the clouds have changed
                              their inscriptions
like cephalopods signing another way of living,
the chimneypots deciphering their markings
don't smoke in this era of central heating
and I expect this spectral encyclopaedia
to evaporate in my vanishing hands.

Anti-climax

The weather warning of thunderstorms
turned out to be little more than a few
passing showers like little sparks
of irritation rather than a full on radgie,
although who would have guessed
the intermittent downpours had slammed
the door and flicked the sneck on the end
of the long, hot summer, but being so
invested in the rapture, in the well-spun
narratives of mass extinction, shell shocked
from the impact of the pandemic
and captivated like a contracted viewer
on Celebrity Gogglebox to the latest
docudrama predicting dystopia –
all those grim freedoms it would bring
just to survive the bloody thing; we stood
around in a fog of bemusement as if
taking in the bitter realisation of being
dumped by text, wondering what
on our ailing mother to do with Autumn,
beckoning at us with its crisped, golding
leaves its bright, plumped, juice-heavy
berries, with the early darkness coming,
slithering out of potholes, drains, gutters,
nooks and crannies from the low lane
with its call for some sort of sacrifice.

Fourth Quarter

"'How beautifully it falls,' you said,
As a leaf turned and twirled
On invisible wind upheld,
How airily to ground
Prolongs its flight."

KATHLEEN RAINE

Lammas Rain

Spitting,
it'll take forever
    to wet
      the pavement,
welcome kisses on bare arms,
    reconfiguring lenses
on spectacles
for microscopic worlds
    like grains
harvested at the height
    of Summer;
our golden days are poured
    into hessian sacks,
hoisted onto shoulders
    lugged into barns,
to be bartered, milled,
baked into crusty loaves.
This mellow rain's
    too light
to formulate a song,
    pigeons applaud
anyway, as if
    it's number one.

Vanishing Points

You know we'll get through this,
we keep reminding ourselves
as Summer closes its curtains
with Winter around the corner,
and the unimaginable numbers
of those who didn't make it this far
into this 'unprecedented' year
disappearing behind us through
the rear-view mirror, over-ripe
brambles still for the picking
straight off the stalk, sweet bombs
of long days we hardly tasted,
wasps drunk on the fullness
of a glorious September's turn.
Don't look back, love. That's my job.
There are mountains all around
and I have no idea how long,
how far, this narrow road will wind.
I'm keeping an eye on the fuel gauge,
we can make it out of here, I'm sure
but the rush of greys, purples, greens
makes me want to cry, or else it's
something we'll not talk about
in clumsy words that can't be trusted
like a loch's thin ice, *sakura*, waterfalls.
Hold my hand between gear changes,
I reckon we'll make it through this year.

Love Me Tender
(For Ian & Justine)

daylight fading,
the voice of the sea climbs
the shelves of shingle,
                turns the air
                into frills of lace
that decorate
          the forests of our lungs;

groynes dip green arms
into the unrelenting swell,
      whilst she
picks through the pebbles
for flotsam:

a shell, a snapped twig,
a lollipop stick, a coil of fishing line,
a straggle of rope

which she fashions
              into a party town
at the foot of the South Downs;

standing in the shallows
of saliva that gather on our tongues
          she squeezes
        salted raindrops
from the corners of our eyes

and all the while
the party people dream
                dub 'n' bass-jazz-garage-house
she'll hang them
                from the pier's end
to catch tomorrow's dawn.

The Jackpot

Recovering, the swelling subsides
outside, leaves have begun to turn
hanging limper, the greens draining
from their tips, as, inside, angry red
fades toward flamingo pink.
The spaces of each day hum
with a hollowness I'm impatient
to fill but the body is its own time
capsule and coils itself up, dips itself
in sleep while fever sweats spin me
through the fruit machine of my years –
childhood toffee apples, grape
heavy mornings, a golden pear
of parenthood, a lemon for letting go.

Film Poem
(based on Peter & The Wolf)

The gate to the meadow hangs off its latch
swings over gravel in the morning wind.

Eerie creak of hinges, someone whining in their sleep
pale face behind stained nets at the windowpane.

What kind of a bird are you that cannot swim?
What kind of a boy are you that cannot fly?

The tabby is prowling around the pond's edge,
the old man watches ghosts from the window.

The tree in the garden stands among fallen apples,
wasps gorge on the tumbled halo of over-ripe fruit.

The mountain's shadow slides across the meadow,
a wolf slinks from the forest's rim, pendulum tongue.

They once hung a witch from the branch of that tree,
what kind of a crone was she that would not sink?

The boy remembers the shudder of the dream,
the old man listens to ghosts from his window.

Last year at the village fair there was a wolf in a cage,
desolate eyes, now it prowls the edges of his sleep.

What kind of a boy are you that will not howl?
What kind of a wolf are you that wears a chain?

The old man is prowling around the pond's edge,
the morning wind stirs the nets at the windowpane.

Drunken wasps gorge upon ghosts in their cages,
stained face behind wolf skin, such desolate eyes.

They once hung a crone from the branch of that tree,
eerie creak of the season like one whining in sleep.

The tabby's shadow slides across the meadow,
they have taken to wearing wolf masks at the fair.

At this time of year the village hangs off its latch,
the boy is wolfing at the shudder of a branch.

It sounds like a duck is quacking inside the old man
who has taken to wearing a halo of freshly fallen fruit.

The gate to the meadow creaks on the edges of sleep
a tree, a rope, a pendulum tongue that refused to sink.

Premonition
(from Kalevala)

I dreamt, last night, of bears and wolves
who crept from the forest and up the stairs
to lick my toes, nuzzle my neck, breathe
their low belly rumbles all over my face,
to paw at my hair and skin, and I whispered,
"Oh, my fair darlings, where've you been?"

But I woke in my bed, alone, to the chorus
of flames, wheezing bellows, to the same
old clatter, the scrape and hammer of iron.

At the edge of the sun-yard, appearing,
vanishing behind white sheets pegged
to the line, standing idle, the young hand
twiddling his thumbs, fingers awaiting
instruction, to occupy his mind, give him
purpose, to distract him from distraction.

I brush my hair. He slaps the back of his neck
and wipes the gnat smudge on his pants.
Hear, the cows lowing, restless in the barn.

Could he resist, if I were still the maid I was,
a glance up to this window, a second, a third –
like the impulsive flight of a nesting bird,
the stirring of insects deep in his stomach,
that dry patch at the back of his throat,
quickening of pulse, a hardening of timber?

A hare is crouched like a boundary stone
by the bramble bushes beside the beck.
I know a tale about a hare on the moon.

I remember those leers from Mid-Summer
parties with wine, the singing and dancing,
swimming, naked, in star-speckled lakes;
the way a hungry bear sniffs at a beehive.
I used to see wolves in the eyes of men
including my husband's, not so long ago.

Once I met a man with a beautiful mind
who could wrestle the harshest weather,
but he was swept away by the black river.

How soon we blend into the backcloth
of tedium, dirty pots, pans, unswept floors,
panel games, soap operas and talk shows
and the daily routine of unfinished chores
that drives me on to pricking my thumbs
with a pin just so I can taste life's tang.

I sing a song my mother once taught me,
how to ask the forest to guard the herd.
Last night I dreamt of wolves and bears.

The Hand of Glory

It's a scorcher
in mid-September,

seven berries dangle
from every branch,

blood stains for the end
of a sacrificial summer

but the 5 o'clock shadows
betray the season,

the way they sprawl
too early, too tar-black

across sun-paled roads,
the way they pool

in potholes and pockmarks
race harvested stubble fields

skritty-scratty like Fred
Flintstones' chinny-chin-chin.

It's all Sex on the Beach.
It's all Slippery Nipples.

It's too bright, too dried
and crisp to go tee-total, or

keep your eyes from squinting
the lids drooping like berries,

lashes locking to stop
your darkness

from leaking out, to resist
sipping from the spring

of slumber and sink into
its pool and while

you wallow, some scally
equipped with a hanged man's

severed hand plucks the giddy-
golden leaves as if they

were Doubloons, Sovereigns,
Threepenny bits, hearts

and other nostalgia-riddled
tokens gone by the bye.

Mabon

Even the tired, tail ends of waves
cling onto the failing daylight
cupping it in their ever-collapsing
curves, which turns the spew
and surf-foam candy-floss pink,
wavelets run from greens to purples
no sign of blue as sanderlings
harangue the incoming tideline,
a flock of flung witch stones.

This familiar coast is perfectly
balanced between the hours
of bright day and dark night;
it's the time of the year to rest,
having brought in the harvest,
to see what it is we have reaped.

I hold onto your hand as we stroll
like a crumpled summer leaf,
fingers chilled by North Sea wind,
nod to the moon as it sails out
from islands of uncharted clouds.

Triangulation

The men stand, talking engines, cylinders,
horsepower, emissions, while the women
at the table discuss gluten intolerances
calories and organic choices. I step out
of the patio door into the closing day,
beyond the garden fence the field stirs,
marks its edges with a line of black trees,
hedges the gliding heron is careful
to ignore. I smoke a roll up, listening
to water trickle into the pond where
carp cruise through reeds with tail-flick,
a billow of fin, oblivious to the party
and hunting heron, the single splash
a chord resounding over rig and furrow.

Local Legend

Maybe I'm on Freya's mound as the bats
emerge on their stretched membranes

out of the trees around Lockwood Beck,
their ultrasonic squeaks and clicks

heralding the Hag's Night around the bend
in the year, to the rhythms of snores –

Arthur still asleep, some hopeful fools say,
to the wash of wind and surf at the foot

of Boulby, and maybe this time round
I won't have to play Grendel although

my eyes do burn with a gruesome light
as wicked dew as e'er my mother knew,

I hear her laughing, a maddening sound
while the bats clothe this hill in night

headlights flicker along the moor's road
and the Jolly Sailor serves frothy pints.

Groundlings

Appearing on the campus green
amid rain-sloshed grass or persistent dew,
the bewilding troops of mushroom heads,
like earth's antennae,

tilt their blind faces
to the sound of footsteps,
twist their necks to catch the vibrations
of passing pundit conversations –

If you look carefully at the guidelines...

Gina was a mess,
but it's hardly her fault...

Will they land a deal?
I've no idea where we stand, and,
to be honest, there's just not enough time....

The way we, me and our kid,
as bairns, would huddle silent on the landing,
after bedtime, ear-wigging for tit-bits
of gossip from the grown-ups downstairs.

With each bulbous skull cap
under-standing the canopy of leaves
as red as harm, or shame, or maybe
the stubborn, hard-to-let-go-of
remnants of trauma;

as if they've shown up for their annual
witness of the tree's reluctant release:

surrender, severance, spiral and landing
the nestling, leaf-shod, suspended
like princes upon sedans borne
by the bent backs of grass blades,

each a treasure relinquished
to the Turning, trophies
from an unrecallable singularity,
apprehended and resoiled by the shrooms.

Walking the Dog

We are treading on the turf roof
of the house of the departed,
taking the leaf coated paths
between gossiping trees whose words
are colours and crinkly textures as if
we are made of wind or breath held
in our balloon skins among the owls
and bats still in hiding, the fur streaks
of squirrels and the posing angels,
Celtic crosses, anchors, fallen pillars
and all the discarded names etched
in stone like shed skin cells, the year
is falling away as a question you wish
you'd asked, a conversation over-
rehearsed in the head but never
managed to mouth, it's always worth
stopping here at the crossways for a kiss,
drop arguments like conkers in casings,
it's like the trees are translating hard-
packed darkness into negative space
and there's nothing else to say... but
I like the feel of the chill evening breeze
on my cheeks as it sweeps us along
like dust toward the wrought iron gates.

Hardraw
"To bear this worthily is good fortune." – Marcus Aurelius

The hills haven't shifted position
while we gazed at our bare hands
but have drawn all around them
rain squalls, retreating behind veils;
green speaks to grey in a dialect
of moss softening fallen boulders
that once formed a farmhouse,
and the great oak on the knoll,
still clutching leaves, surveys the vale,
the river-soaked floodplain meadows
of hawkbit, sneezewort, toadflax,
the potholed track up to the village.

A red squirrel pays a visit, his fur
drenched spikes – punk rocker
pogoing along the dry-stone wall,
to stop and stand stock still eyeing
me up, just yards away and I ask
in a sing-song voice, *Who killed Bambi?*

The guttering's been overflowing
for most of the wrung-out day,
rain lashing the windows,
hammers the corrugated roof,
huffs, puffs at the door of our hut,
driven by a hereditary blood feud,
all night it'll roar through the dale
from waterfalls surging in vats
of curdled cream, along the lane
down from Simonstone, High Shaw,

from the stone ridges and open fell,
comes the wayfarer, Joe, who, some
whisper, has walked from Arimathea,
bent-backed, striding through puddles
with his twisted beechwood stick,
the old dote's got sommat to prove,
from his curled, whiskered lip
hang both a blessing and a curse,
and though this whittling weather
despises the idea of monuments,
delights in the desecration of icons

the Oak King, regardless, is gathering
his crows to his gloom, the last one
to let go of the lighter patches of sky,
hoarding its leftover slivers of rainbows
with the tenacity of a Yorkshire-bred
green dragon kale-eyed on Old Peculier.

If you ventured out to stand beside it
you'd hear it creaking, boughs rattling
your feet would feel its grip on earth,
your face stung by the prick of raindrops
as if water had set to sharp steel pins
shaped by heat and pressure and touching
its wet bark you would come to know
what withstanding means, rooted, reaching,
holding, protecting, wholly dependable,
sprung from the cold darkness of the soil,
progeny of the primeval forest, guardian
and giver, and as stoicism is about more
than simple survival, regal and reciprocal.

Samhain

I am at the threshold of the open door
Waiting for my wary guest to appear
Stepping through the cold downpour,
I can sense her presence drawing near.

Come, Love, there's nothing to fear.
I've already carved and lit the pumpkin
See, how its grin glows from ear to ear,
See, the veil between us has grown thin.

This house is ready to receive my dear
With incense of nutmeg, cloves, myrrh.
She will tell me tales I'm keen to hear
Her Summer stories will bring me cheer.

As she tastes a seed from a pomegranate
I shall drain a full glass of dark Diablo,
Squeezing our days like ripened grapes
She'll bide with me in smoke and shadow.

Burning the Bones

Even though it's only Midday,
and the patch of sky through the window
framing the rooftop and chimney pots
of the house opposite is a worn-out,
scuffed blue denim, the long night
is congregating on the Northern hinds
of our homes, in the lee of land's
rolling folds, biding its time under piles
of abandoned leaves dotting the pavements
like the mounds of hastily dug graves.
The clouds bring updates from over the pond.

We cross our fingers and hope for the best,
while the stacked banefires of timber
wait for the spark to consume our effigies,
turn heroes and villains into flakes of swirling ash.
And the daughter signing her name
with a sparkler on the brisk air's register,
reads the afterglow through a plume of breath,
as the acorns of this mast year,
tanned leather bullets
are trodden into their Winter beds,
their radicles eager to root, hollering,
Now wait a while,
just wait, some of us shall rise.
And our piths draw strength from the soil.

Wild-Route

hill frost
        a dampened tissue
        sprawled
                over undulations
the copse is an ancient
        crown of twistings
                to catch
lace-tails of draughts
     dreamings
ululations
on bare bark fingers

there is, as always, a road
        sweeping
                headlights
on tarmac   grit
black ice
the quick way home…

hear,
        the rush-hush of its song
silences almost everything
                but itself –
a mating call to its neighbours
        across the rolling
                slopes
of hemmed in fields…

Sunder   Seaham,
Shotton   Seaton

the land shivers behind fences
       the waves recoil
              out of reach
the black snakes encircle
hill, wood, beck, vale
       I ride
their backs
       wondering if,
       between them, there are still
lesser routes
and corpse ways to venture.

Headland

Edge of land;
the sea is riding
two horses:

one gallops forward

headlong into
an unknowable
tomorrow,

the other races
back

drawn by
a craving to that
which wears

an illusion of
familiarity,

the hooves churn
up shingle

send
plumes spitting
high

where gulls
circle grey, coal
stained

wingtips
against November's
nutty slack clouds

faces raw
as slapped arses

the waves are wild,
folding

years within
their bottomless
drawers,

turning
keep-sakes in
chilled fingers

that rummage
into every crevice,

plucking surf flowers
in lily white
bouquets

the bitter wind
sharpens the teeth

of the wolf
that growls at the door
of our straw houses

have you noticed
how the evenings
come

spilling
from the bellies
of breakers

to dash themselves
apart on the piers?

That's how, these days,
it's already dark by four.

Head of the Heathen
(Pen-y-Ghent)

The dry-stone wall runs on forever and a day
over sleet-drenched pens

like a long, hard squint at the horizon-line
from a seat of ease, the ground

dips and rolls in awakening colours,
a mirage of land far out

on some uncharted sea, peat-black hollows,
moor-grass on every crest,

but days are scraped back to a few good hours
to traverse meadows and tend

to the livestock, keeping an eye on the blaze
of sky to the west. Deep country:

spills, rakes, plunges and trends,
the waters wonderous cold,

singing bored caves in the bubbling
darkness through millstone grit,

carboniferous limestone, to burst from earth
at Brants Gill Head. These blokes

knaa well how t' cling ont' turf when the sky
decides to swallow them whole.

They're muttered superstitions for what it's worth,
the argot of earth, indecipherable oghams

scratched on a menhir. Serious dominoes
clacking in the bar beside the hearth's

throbbing embers, half-downed pints, their eyes
high soaring buzzards surveying scrublands.

Christ on a Stick

Either it was
a high gravity day
or else
he'd run out of usable spoons
which was annoying
as he had been so very careful
all day
yesterday to conserve
as best he could
each lip-brimmed bowlful
of life...
measuring out the expected
expenditure of energy
required to manage the ordinary
day to day,
spoon to spoon, activities
that most conduct without
as much as a second thought:

- Three tablespoons to climb the stairs
- Two cream soup spoons to get dressed
- One salt spoon to reach for the remote;

but with this wet November's late afternoon
squatting on his slumped shoulders
standing on the station platform
minding the gap
the drop

trying to stem the leakage
from the tip of his numb nose
and the tips of his toes
he realised that all along
he must have been using
a tarnished sieve-spoon,
a tea strainer, an olive spoon or
a wooden honey spoon
instead of
something sensible like a ladle
carved from horn, tusk or bone
dating back beyond the Egyptians
to the dawn of the Palaeolithic.
Christ on a stick! The gift,
catch and cradle his melt! Even
one of the many brown-edged
sycamore leaves lying underfoot
scooped up and cupped in a palm
would have been more use
than ornament to get
him home.

Pheasants in Porvoo Snow

They emerge   like fugitives,
with tentative paces   upon
the whitened track   as we might
traverse a frozen lake, stepping
from snowflake onto compacted
            snowflake   attuned to
the groans of trapped air-pockets.

They keep to the cover of the evergreen
hedge, twitching heads this way then
the other,   clocking   the spaces
for threats: the empty road,
the ice-locked ditch   the leafless
patient trees, our branches   weigh
heavy on our brows as   we   tread
in a procession through forest-mouldering
apples   toad-stools   fallen stars

our masks   beginning   to slip;
through eye-holes   we spot
their mottled feathers, quick flashes
of a russet neck   note how near
they stay   so as to sense the warm
         symmetry
                  of one another's tremors
beneath the bowl of a glass-blown sky,
painted freshly this borrowed morn
in pink   in peach   and mauve.

Brief Visitor

Cocooned in the armchair by the window,
profile traced by winter sun, uncertainty
testing the density of the present
against the membrane of our futures, it gives
slowly, slightly, little by little; she sighs
in self-doubt at her capability to shift
into the shapes of this year's expectations
but determined to try, let herself evolve
and bear the flowers and fruits of each
accumulating month toward their term.
No longer a child, she is still my bairn
although today just paying a visit,
she doesn't live here anymore; I'm quiet,
listening for the star she's begun to grow.

Unrealing Ontology, 2016

In the tower he was talking talking about
unreliable narrators, pointing out the very real
possibility of a boy selling himself to those men
for the price of a pair of Nike trainers and whether
the girl on the bus was real at all or just a reflection
until his eye drifted to the window, the fast trail of smoke
from the chimney over the river, crossing a smudge of pink sky
in absolute denial, the glints of lights, night coming in;
Christmas just around the corner with the dark angel
in his empty exhibition earthbound by the memory
of signing on in that very room – writing rewriting
a page from a story, 'what does the reader know?'
but his wife, he said, had told him she was sick,
and so I tell Chris who flies, at last, to Finland tomorrow,
that he knows, deep down, that everything
outside the town is just a hologram anyway...

Driftwood

Topsy turvy, semi-transparent
she's formed from foam and fret
but she's smiling up at the charcoal
splotches blanketing the wee bay
though the day is cold and wet.

The southern cliff is a sleeping dragon,
its woods scored by burns that pour
along its scales, they say the sea-hag's
long gone although one day she'll return
once all the shanties have been sung.

A cloud of gannets harasses a coble
and haar has gobbled up the horizon,
here between the greens and greys
among cuts, wynds, holiday homes,
the mizzle spins history into fable.

The baby has gone without being born,
neither of us can speak its name, she's
on the breakers' rocks slick with runoff
from incoming billows, she's beneath
the never-steady surface of the churn.

She's made of bubbles, swirling sands,
eroded shell, mermaids' purses, and
she tells me, how she just loves the sea!
We watch it like an animated movie
like the ones she likes by Studio Ghibli.

The Reunion

The truth of the situation
lies in the not-saids, in the way
conversations skirt so skilfully,
almost effortlessly, around
those questions that could
carry too much weight, prove
too pointed to answer calmly;
they move smooth as house cats
between calves and chair legs
hungry for dropped crumbs.

How we all, out of a sense
of delicacy and prudence, keep
firmly to the immediate, focus
fastidiously on the minutiae
of detail, relying upon the hard
and fast directions of the known
and mutually agreed upon (as
there's much we don't) – new
shoes for instance, the days off
for those in regular jobs,
and wouldn't it be just lovely
to have another white Christmas,

I mean when was the last,
can anyone remember, it must
have been before...oh never mind....

Given there are so many dead
ends we have become adept
at skating over the gathering's
thin ice, ignoring the depths below
while holding the mysteries
we have wrapped and swapped
in shiny paper which everyone,
but the bairns, is hesitant to open,
for, like the answers to our unasked
questions, remind us of who
isn't there, and maybe more
importantly, the whys, and the price
of each unmentionable absence.

Meeting the *Cailleach*

I've watched the darkness swell
to smother spaces and distances
as we hurtle towards the solstice,
and I have stridden through it, slipping
along damp paths between graves,
ground mist, its clammy chill, and forgot,
in the haste to reach home, to linger
within its shivering potential, to take
a little time to sample its treasure,
let it press upon me the weightlessness
of wintering, so now I cannot help
but stop dead in my tracks, frozen,
for some odd reason distraught by
the glow of windows and streetlamps.

Herd

There are places beyond the perimeter of this waterlogged field where minds are mashed with a bitter brew of misplacement, the tug and tow of the tide has turned the truth inside out like a cockerel's innards spread to interpret which way tomorrow will fall, there are changes occurring, transfers of power along with the inevitable backlash, past's drag putting the brakes on progression, it doesn't matter too much that it's started to pour, the ground has turned into a quagmire and the public footpath is impassable, although you guys don't seem to mind too much about the best route out of the knee-deep mud having accepted your lot to stand and stare at anything that moves in the squall: cliff-top ghosts, hooded pilgrims, black-eyed wind-tossed crows dissolving into cataract whiteness, wind strums the wire fence, rain drips from your horns, you huddle like a henge of stones, impassive as I decide to backtrack the trail past the unlit farm.

Dunking for a New Sun

This earth's longest night
roams the backstreets,
winds down country lanes
to where roads peter out,
the wind teases tears from eyes –
a child crying in the darkness,
we move inside,
edge deeper into the cave,
the candle lit corners,
watching the flicker
bring our pictures to life,
we have brought in the wild forest,
poison berries, pinecones, stars
the gathering of a year's spent seconds,
shuffle cards, toss the die, roll the ball
drink, eat, kindle the sparks
between us
while we wait
for the orange to resurface
from the bucket's swilling waters.